Half-Dreaming

poems

Douglas Nordfors

Half-Dreaming

poems

Douglas Nordfors

Plain View Press, LLC
1101 W 34th Street, STE 404

www.plainviewpress.net
Austin, TX 78705

Copyright © 2020 Douglas Nordfors. All rights reserved under International and Pan-American Copyright Conventions. No part of this book may be reproduced or distributed in any form or by any means, or stored in a data base or retrieval system, without written permission from the author. All rights, including electronic, are reserved by the author and publisher.

ISBN: 978-1-63210-070-2
ebook ISBN: 978-1-63210-071-9
Library of Congress Control Number:2019956144

Cover art by Beverly Goodrum
Cover design by Pam Knight

We Find Healing In Existing Reality
Plain View Press is a 40-year-old issue-based literary publishing house. Our books result from artistic collaboration between writers, artists, and editors. Over the years we have become a far-flung community of humane and highly creative activists whose energies bring humanitarian enlightenment and hope to individuals and communities grappling with the major issues of our time—peace, justice, the environment, education and gender.

Contents

ABSTRACT   9
    Children's Poem   11
    Inorganic   13
    Detail Study   15
    First Love   16
    Sonnet   17
    The Valley of   18
    To a Stranger   19
    The Life of the Mind   20
    A Dream   21
    Modern Romance   22
    Pre-Valentine's Day Poem   23
    The Not Me   24
    A Question   25

CONCRETE   27
    The Foundation   29
    The Process   31
    Pigeon   32
    A Pop Song   33
    The Young Man   34
    The House Where We Used to Live   35
    A Visitor   36
    Exterior Interior Monologue   38
    A Walk Through Central Park   39
    Forgivable   40
    Her Garden   41
    Where I Live   43
    Gone Now   45

ABSTRACT   47
    The Days of My Birth   49
    Symphony in One Movement   50
    Monday Morning Logic   51
    Deliberate Ecstasy   52
    Self-Portrait   54
    Metaphysical Siblings   55
    Prime Dream   56
    Tabula Rasa   57
    In No   58
    Each Stage   59
    The Collected Poems of Chris Waterson   60
    Journal Entry   63

CONCRETE   65
    August 4, 2014   67
    The Reagan Era   68
    October 24, 1929   70
    Waiting for a Bank Machine   71
    The IRS   72
    As I Apply for a Job   73
    Self-Help   74
    My Weekday Morning Routine   75
    Aftereffect   76
    Two Months After the Partial Clear-Cutting
          Across the Road from My House   77
    Forecast   78
    Poem to a Friend   79

Acknowledgments   81
About the Author   83

Wholeness is not achieved by cutting off a portion of one's being, but by integration of the contraries.

—Carl Jung

There is no energy unless there is a tension of opposites.

—Carl Jung

ABSTRACT

Children's Poem

Fractious forces
pulled the tide
under,

and tied it to
seahorses'
necks, strings

of them, with blue
pieces of
kelp with

white and black pearls
bedecked. Such
hard words

to look up, to
solve as if
they were

fractions. May not
be always
what you

expect, syntax—
follow it
to the

end, and then go
backwards up
to make

sure you see the
clearness. Not
a sin

at all to tax
your mind. One
seahorse

is yours, and still
rhymes with the
others

inside your in-
terior,
for sure.

Your tongue is en-
jambed, but not
your heart,

if you read it
and feel it
right, this

string of stanzas
and abstract
matter

that's made nothing
happen. Well
on its

way the tide is,
like an extra
syllable,

and then another,
like another day
nearly done.

Why
so many people can't
see the moon

the moon
need not explain.

Inorganic

Some days, the sun goes down, and something goes wrong.

What? The skin around my eyes
tenses like a muscle,
waiting
for a disembodied animal
or vegetable nerve to touch,
waiting
for a reservoir
to sink a carved notch, for the knife point
at which pipes under a city
will get lost in their own maze, and some substance
completely resembling tap water will
come down out of the tap and stop
with a flick of the wrist.

Is it one of those days? Perhaps
inside a cage inside a body, an animal
doesn't moan at the barred sunlight. Perhaps
above the cage, the dumb stars breathe hard,
and the grass, wherever lit green is,
longs, like a petal (on a table absent from a room)
swept into a cupped hand,
to fall.

What do I know? Life is shades
of one aggrieved, candy-colored mood, some nights,
as the moon goes down
through matter and crux and dark air,
isn't it? And is it
one of those nights?

Consolidate. Like an animal gathering its flying
everywhere to make materials
to make a nest, consolidate—

is this vegetable or mineral
voice, hard as fire,
mine?

What I don't know, I think,
is telling me that there are times I need not
try not to float
in the intervals between inescapable occurrences.

Other days, the sun goes down.

Detail Study

I've been reduced to life, specifically
to a human shape
worn down,
and now
I can say I want
to watch the sun like a hawk or a falcon or an astronomer
wavering, unbidden,
toward solar shores breaking the system
of waves
of light,

an astronomer
with ten or five bare
fingers treading the steps
of the air like a doctor or a lawyer or a carpenter,
welcome only
to the initial pinnacle of the sky,
as a falcon,
like a telescope removing itself
from an eye, turns back, trying to decide
who I've become,

and settles on
my gloved wrist.

First Love

The loneliness I felt, yes,
was the loneliness she felt.

We spent our youths,
before we came to be,

looking out a window
containing no reflection,

only the city outside:
old sidewalks like unfinished

cathedrals, streets paved
dark, yellow lines, telephone poles

like trees, branches and leaves
taken away to a safe place—

we knew not where.

Once, just after we met,
she averted her eyes,

and the yellow, separating
lines remained, and

the sidewalks stopped cracking
open—there was nothing

to reveal. The window
was dark. And then her eyes

turned back to me, and then
beneath me I wasn't.

Over cathedral sidewalks
was the answer

to where the sun shone.

Sonnet

Who is this person I want to be?
To stretch to within his illimitable
limbs do I have the capacity?
Is being becoming, or is what I'm after
diminishment, as death is capable
of taking surfaces upon waves of laughter
and turning them into one tide of pathos?
Images, especially poor ones, aren't
receptive to truth when I have to ask,
when who I want to be doesn't rhyme
with who I am. Here is my ideal ethos:
My intimate, lonely twins, shyness and fear,
share last laughs before and after leaving
the shore of a poor land and abandoning

me to opportunity.

The Valley of

I take the child inside me back to a place far,
far below the sky.

There's a house there with a place for fire,
fire after a spark,

like an ax, makes kindling out of a stump rounder
than any tree ring.

All over the place are tall plants widening
as they fall, tall plants

being planted some time after a seed
conceived the child, and

the child a seed. Beyond the place, life
only goes forward,

so it goes, and beyond the stone garden
path in the viewless

back yard, a hearth can't conceive a new heart,
so it, the old heart,

goes on being a child, not quite living up to
its latter self.

No rooms to breathe.
Front window after front window looks out at

fences, fences
building more fences with tall pieces of thick

kindling, and now
it's time to reach the end, the end stagnant,

one more word, just
one more word, before the shadow of.

To a Stranger

I come out from behind the walls of my house
and stand in my front yard
and imagine
that the pear tree in bloom is a gift from you.

The street beyond the fence goes both ways
and is completely quiet.

Last evening, I sat next to you on the bus.
You looked sad and incomplete.
Your raincoat promised rain and your purse
held itself shut like a mouth.

When I got up to let you out,
I wondered where we were, glanced all the way
out the window and saw
street signs crossing paths at the top of a pole.

The doors opened and you began walking home.
Maybe there was no one for you
to come home to.
Maybe

you had nothing in your power
to give but a pear tree in bloom
on a street you have never seen.

You shouldn't have.

The Life of the Mind

I am walking along thinking
that every waiter and clothesline
and fashion model and school bus
and clown and milk carton and cop
and Laundromat I've ever seen
were created to inspire me
to love them, when, out of the blue,

everyone and everything
leaves me cold, when, out of the blue,
I am walking along thinking
that thinking is hopeless. And then
I have the sensation I am
home, breathless, wringing a downpour
out of my clothes. And then I realize

that nothing has actually happened.
I am walking along thinking
that love never dies.

A Dream

In a great silence,
I am in your hands,

walking on acres of pavement
within a slum

where the strongest child screams
out the breath

that keeps him alive
among the old men

who loiter outside the little store
as if succeeding in returning to themselves

like the only sun.

It is not your beauty.
It is not your mind as large

as the stains of another existence.
It is not the dream of rankness and air.

It is that you are here,
shedding the hard center of the world

like weather from the muscle
of child and man,

waiting for me to burn my gentleness down
to graceless longing,

and then touch you.

Modern Romance

Leaning on no one
prepares me
for actuality. Actuality
doesn't take
permanently. Eventually,
the voice of no one calls me,
and I go.

I need her, and I need her
to be free of me.
Before I return,
the voice of no one is
Earth with nothing
in it, save a plant, maybe
a foxglove, maybe
a cyclamen, plants
I've heard of, plants I believe
I've never seen.

Before I return,
with her hands
in a bed with nothing
in it, save a flower,
she just wants
to hear the sound of
her own voice, the beat of
her own mind.
I need him, I need him. Three words
forming the sort of thought
only ones
who feel bereft
entertain.

Pre-Valentine's Day Poem

Our seasoned, not yet cold heart
is, to my naked eyes, as
viable as peeled-off bark standing apart
from its tree, is as yet

not real, and works the way
a wild, evolving metaphor or simile
works, and works its way, like
love, with such unbelievable patience, into

a biological soul, while a mouth
from a practiced, imminent kiss stands
apart, the exposed skin on such
sure lips as yet not even

tasting the air, and I try
to breathe in while telling you
all this all the time, even
with my eyes closed.

The Not Me

has the right to cross-fertilize
with the pollen in and around
its eye-corners even before
the me myself dies and turns
the literature of spring's
pages left or right—if I knew

what I was saying, I would
breed superabundant eyes,
and pour their plain, plain water,
the precise opposite of
flower dust, into sockets
scooped into personal bone.

A Question

What is life? It took billions of years
for a question to get to me and no time
to flow like breath into my mouth. Now

comes the need to answer it, the fear the
need creates. Waiting to answer it
is like going through the stages of grief

before a death creates the need to grieve.
While waiting, I imagine a crow flying back
and forth over a field of snow, one white

mitten lying somewhere on the surface.
Then, still waiting, I imagine a paradise,
a bare orchard lost in the thought that

it's still alive. Then I stretch to pick,
my other hand pressing on my elbow
to keep it locked, my hands like unknown

languages, the answer translated forth
and back, the crow in my head mindful
of how my imagination outdistances my feeling

that my courage is on its way to me still.

CONCRETE

The Foundation

The only sandcastle on the whole beach
is unmindful of who it is.
Hands built it.
Small hands. Or created it
out of sand created out of the mind of who?
And out of salt water
sliding back into the ocean as if building back
into a wave.

All this
means nothing, perhaps,
is like
a detail that no one can see
in a movie that no has seen,
shrouded
as it is
and as the movie is
in cinematography and human costumes,
or like
an undescribed image
in a missing book missing
a vital word,
"castle"
or "sand".

Is it
medieval
or timeless?
It speaks for itself, as they
who are
no one say.

And then a child
comes as if into the camera frame
to see, and to not see,
his handiwork, her handiwork.
Two identical hands,
and then four identical
ankle-high walls,

like the foundation
of endless skyscrapers,
no, degenerated sand,
no, broken brain waves
that no one has heard of,
that everyone has heard.

The Process

We said our goodbyes.
She left my apartment and
climbed down the stairs.
There came to be a time
when I looked out the window
and watched her walk away.

I said goodbye again,
this time to a raised drawbridge
as transparent as glass
and the size of a small window.
And this time to a sky
so itself there was no

place in it for clouds
I said goodbye again.
Ahead of her on the sidewalk
a moat as shallow as
a sheet of glass and
the size of a pool of rain.

There came to be a time
when she reached the other side
in one long stride.
Come up short
she did not, yes,
one of her feet did not

drown and resurrect
itself in the process.

Pigeon

As if I was looking up at one pigeon in the vast flock
at my feet, I distinctly remember
standing in winter in a tiny city park and feeling
that my unique notion that my sole
wool coat, and not the general human capacity for shielding
ourselves, was why I was indifferent
to the cold. I distinctly remember being neither
a young man nor a man—a crude

balancing act as if parallel to no one—and chafing
my bare hands together, and being aware
that I wasn't kneeling down and praying: May I grow
to lose my characteristic illusions,
and look at all the glassy eyes my eyes mirror, and see
the multiplied, mistakable beauty,
the blanket human language that, like a mother and a father,
gave them their name.

A Pop Song

On the radio a woman is singing the line,
"I never meant to hurt you."
In her voice is
a useless sobbing
I've come to believe is
one of the things I breathe in to stay alive.

I don't know, I hate this song
but I desire this woman
to sing to me, to remind me
we hurt each other because we don't
know our own strength.

It must be almost over—she's repeated
"I never meant to hurt you"
so many times it could be the only
line anyone's ever been given.
The only question is,

this person she never meant to hurt,
how fluid is his life
now that he knows the rain never
meant to strike his eyes
and slide down his cheeks?

I see him pacing back and forth in a garden,
talking to the stone animals,
enduring their closed
throats and ears.
What does he want from her?

He wants her to lead him out of the garden
and pick flowers with him along the side of the road.

The Young Man

Once, as we stood in the airy space
between our houses, my neighbor
said, "I call this house the graveyard,"
meaning her house, and meaning
she had lived in it through the deaths
of her husband and all of her friends—
I knew this from less desperate, less poetic

things she had, at other times, said.
I must have wondered, as we stood
in the airy space, if a metaphor
made up of many little houses
marked with headstones was too little
or too much, and I wonder now
if the young man, inside me still,

had a heart, meaning did I, before
I moved away, in a waking dream
walk onto her front yard, and on
her doorstep lay a few flowers,
so that, opening, not expecting
them, she would throw them out
or stumble over them, and begin again?

The House Where We Used to Live

On bare paper I write:

As if birth could not help
but not change me
into someone, as if I am
the world and me without
me, I am a wide eye
shutting as it closes

on another eye that
sees merely a candle
on a nightstand, all I
remember of one room,
not to mention a bare
floor and four walls as bare as

paper. Merely? A candle
that, burning or not, as each
successive night slowed,
lit up the noncircular
lines, the circumference, both
more than visible, of her

body and mine, of her
body and the world, as,
standing on a night,
kneeling, first light
slowed and stopped.

A Visitor

Come in, just
throw your coat over there, have some tea, be careful,

it's hot. I'm sorry,
I'm getting ahead of myself. Take your coat off, and I'll

boil some water,
soon, after my nerves have nearly died down.

Because I don't know
where beauty lives, I see in your face an unoccupied house.

No, that's wrong. No,
that painting was painted by my father, before I was born.

You'd rather die
than leave? There's no point in coming so far

for no reason.
I left you in the living room for a while, and here's your tea,

be careful, your lips
are beautifully cold, the weather got to them,

the outside weather
I can see in your eyes, in windows, living windows

throughout my house.
How did I get a cup of tea, too? Two I must have made,

or you made one
for me, somehow, when I wasn't looking.

How can that be?
Are you content? I am. I mean I'm trying to be,

thinking my own thoughts
in the dim light of the strangeness of not knowing yours.

On the surface
we're talking about things. I 'm waiting for you

to ask me
about the painting, and to say you find your tea to be

as miraculous,
though not as hot, as the sun. My house

is a cosmos.
"Yes and no," you say when I ask you how you are.

"What do you mean?"
I say, and you say, "What do you mean what do you mean?"

Now I feel wonderful
because I'm confused now on the whole surface

as well as below mine.

Exterior Interior Monologue

I'm walking alone around the center
of town this evening, after, inside
my house outside the center of
town, a friend told me about
her long-dead grandfather, a furniture maker.
I must have imagined, as I
listened, that out of kindness she
offered me a piece of cloth
that then lay on my outstretched
palm, and then told me to
make it into something new, after
first holding it, growing old into
its form already ending in death,
and then I walked alone to
the center of town, and here
I am, walking around. I must
have imagined that I was hungry,
that I wanted to enter a
nice restaurant with tablecloths I and
her grandfather made. No, my mind,
now that it has from her
parted, can't in the same vein
go on.

A Walk Through Central Park

The breeze gently lowers you, lowers
me to the ground, lifts us up, grass stains on our knees

and lips. There's something about
this place that makes me want to

invent our lives. It occurs to me
that everyone here, from the old woman

feeding crumbs to pigeons to the little girl
roller skating backwards to the horror

of her mother, is surviving this moment,
preparing even now for the next,

their strenuous hearts as unshaken
as the future. I tell you a subdued version

of what occurred to me. You tell me
you were thinking the exact same thing.

We pass a man in a heavy sweater
sitting cross-legged on a bench, staring

at nothing as if at a web strung between
two pillars of air. "Listen," you think. "Listen,"

I think, "tomorrow it'll be cold again, and tonight
I'll enter your body: what I am in all weather."

We've thought of how sunlight falls to the pavement
like rain, gathers in the gutters, slides toward the grates.

But today we think of how sunlight falls without
disturbing the grass. Though we're wary

of our imagination that claims sunlight
was once tangible and unreal, we think of how

everything is so much better now and forever.

Forgivable

In that way I have, I imagine
that the sand-colored horse on this beach
in Maine walking between a man
and a woman walking uneasily
over the sand, reins slack in one hand,
the woman's, cannot suffer itself,
is a third hand rolling in endless
waves out beyond salt and water,
mane drowning, spine afloat, four legs
purposely drifting and kicking.

And now that I'm close enough, I see
the man's only eyes, dead ahead and
yet searching around for a wild, idle
image of love, pointing sideways through
neck muscles, through hide and skull, searching
for the other side, where she dwells—
I see a man and a woman together not so much
implicating as improbably
symbolizing the horse, its loose bridle
both a circle and its circumference,

over its back a dark blanket
that can't, of course,
stop the light rain from falling.

Her Garden

Saint Francis of Assisi,
watch over her garden, and not just because
there's a small stone statue of you inside it.
Somewhere, the garment you wear the play

of wind can animate, the weather can't decay.
I'm trying to sing your eyes downward,
so to speak, while, as if in the lapses
of time only you have the power to see,

different kinds of birds alight on your crown.
Yes, it's her garden, and hers alone. You see,
we live together, but I have no aptitude.
Once, I asked her what she wanted to grow. "Oh, you know,"

she said, addressing you, rather than me,
I believe. "Tulips," she went on to say, "pansies,
hyacinths, red roses, tomatoes, eggplants,
and then, summer over, black-eyed Susans,

mums, dahlias, broccoli, Brussels sprouts
and more." A small stone statue, and between
stone-bordered plots a stone path leading
everywhere, save to the small city and the din

of traffic on speechless roads, she didn't say.
Saint Francis of Assisi, before winter
turns to flesh, allow her to allow herself
inside her garden, knowing in her heart

that it will melt like water once again,
while from the earth, not restored but renewed
like an unruined church, and from the sky,
you create a world where dogs and wolves

are friends, where to a man like me a woman is abundance,
where two people whose power of speech is more than faint...
Saint Francis of Assisi,
allow us from our level vantage point

to turn to each other in the tall, tall shadow
of your only slightly inexact likeness,
and say, "I love you," and "I love you, too."

Where I Live

I'm beginning to feel
the lamentations
at the forefronts of
funeral homes, to see
the lines of houses
beyond the vacant landscapes,

I'm ending up at birth
constructed out of
wood or redeemed trees
or bricks glued together
with nails, I'm beginning

to trim the dumb
anguish from
my fingernails and let them grow
until it's time,

I'm ending,
in myself only,
the songs of songbirds settled

on a branch covering
two back yards, or on

power lines, by not allowing

emotion to fly off
into tangents—not all

ballads hit a wall
like a knuckle
and can't come in, I'm

beginning
to listen to
the lines
of dogwood trees between

competing gas stations
and edible supermarkets,
to breathe, to
feel, in the light, the pressure
of a hand

on my backbone as the hand extends
all the way home
to my mother and father standing
on the horizon
in the house
with no back door.

Gone Now

Many times, my mother told me
not not to cry,
but that I did not cry
when I was born.

Just science, or
astrology (or an unnamed
twofold field of study)
manifesting itself.

Still, at this juncture
of my life, out of that first juncture
I need to try
to make more.

Was it actually a demand, my hushed,
undivided acceptance of life,
after as well as before the cord was cut?
A demand for what? Did silence clarify? Did further silence

cleanse the hard life I had yet to scratch the surface of?
Did established silence, as it struck me
that I could breathe, into a powder
grind my throat, a powder not

so fine that it couldn't be reversed,
that my potential
vocal cords were an omen of the physical world?
Or was I, in effect, a completed

cadence, a resounded sound looking through
the world for dry images of the set distances from farm
to farm evolving into the peaceful city
where I was born?

In my own nameless world,
supremely ignorant of all but love's conceit,
I believe my mother, gone now, in so many words, in the throes
of the mother of all wisdom generated,

but not bound, by facts,
was telling me that the day of my death
will, without a plea for answers,
or a cry for questions, arrive.

ABSTRACT

The Days of My Birth

This morning, for instance, I let the rain fall,
as if in it I had
a hand,

for help

appealing neither to gravity nor to
my unraised, unphased
spirits.

Symphony in One Movement

Major undertaking, Allegro
in the huge distance, and also Allegro
wondering, as if music itself
can wonder, why it wasn't planted
in the beginning, and why here, now,
exists something like autumn
extreme heat, melted blood
going from key to key in a clearly
sad, somewhat vigorous rhythm,
no instruments, or at least
no metal, no cymbals or symbols, Grave
representing Largo just because it can,
no, not even something like autumn extreme heat,
seasonless, as opposed to a seasonal
hybrid, yes, Adagio or Andante
alone, the distance major, huge
and nowhere in the distance, cold
and the concept of
cold like lips exchanging
motion with a closed mouth and
a closed mouth breaking apart
from lips in a rhythm ending
and beginning eternally gratefully
on a note of minor hope.

Monday Morning Logic

Worrying, as I listened
to rain take care of itself
outside my walls and curtained windows,
about money,

I was awake,
but I lay still. I'd like to say
that rain dropped down from the indifferent universe,
but, though

the sound of rain couldn't hear me,
I seemed to matter,
I, myself, seemed
to grow the wealth I needed, while on healthy trees

money gave off
an air of,
or gave away,
dignity—

did it matter which? I'd like to say
that trees, in a dream,
took me back to when a forest was freedom,
to where poached deer guilty

of living were consumed
in peace, to where
deer were beautiful, and that's that,
but, though

it couldn't see itself, the sound of rain
clearly
dropped down,
and so I rose.

Deliberate Ecstasy

can't help but
proceed in fragments:

Dejection, once
kicked in,
kisses ashes.

And again.

Words that instantly
break in ideas, as opposed to
slowly and painfully break forth into
visual images, are
my fruitless preference.

But life. But life,
in many ways,
is a partial whole.

Is like
the image
of a forbidden deity.

Once and again, I
pronounce
lips almost literally, almost sacredly
turn to them and to them
turn, until
flesh they are.

Until a closed,
flesh-colored tongue stuck in behind them
rejects dejection, and
drifts like gray sparks, gray, sifted-though
syllables, down
to the foot of a throat,
and up.

At
the same time, finally
my consciousness
arouses
the dregs of the bile
of pale happiness,
the dim signs of greater happiness
that don't not pale
in comparison so much as
speak, and eventually

in split tongues, sing.

Self-Portrait

A face without a hand
painted.

A body with
the motion inherent in a brush
permeating every other corner on one
utterly blank canvas, and another.

That's not enough.

An arm—
embrace it, and it
out of love
makes...

That's it.

There could be
another arm, besides the one
I haven't mentioned.

That's not enough.

Fused knees
with and without flesh and blood.
Consciousness flowing like a vine and like
a vein up to the heart of a brain.

A mind—
cling to it, and it puts blind trust in a mouth
and an ear to the embodiment
of the ground.

Eyes
like diffuse cheekbones meeting
anyone who could be.

Metaphysical Siblings

Upon learning that my brother, who isn't
me, reached the summit of Mount Rainer,
a summit I'll never reach, I try to

take stock of the situation. I want to stop
thinking of conjunction, because a valley
isn't a cavity in the earth, which makes

complete, unclear sense. I want to
do only what I can do, which is to distinguish
a world from the world in me. In me, who is

taller than my brother, a snow-capped hill
is Mount Rainer, or isn't until I undertake
the short, credibly invigorating climb.

Prime Dream

For months, I haven't seen a sunset.
For months, I've seen the sun
begin to fall. A horizon
hovers over this womb
with its nine moons
orbiting around
eight fingernails, mine
if the sun sees me
sink or swoon.

I know, already, what it means to ascend
depleted into
being and
nonbeing. Rubbing into, just
that simple idea,
engenders salt water and cracked lips,
yet simply slipping
on a patch of ice presupposes caution,
the motion of evasion.

This womb must go down past the depth
from which it rose,
and if I desire to see, within
the sun's cycle,
a rose
or a cyclamen,
this womb
must go without me.

Tabula Rasa

Forget at birth—my mind becomes a blank slate
again and again,
and again and again my mind fills with entirely
new material,
abstract and abstruse. For instance, it's so easy
to reach out and rest
my finger on the light purple flower in the vase
on the table—no,
it would be if water and air didn't feel
half-full—no, if
hitting home wasn't circuitous, torturous—no,
if I could, like
an inverted painter, paint the table on the vase,
the restive dark
in the rootless light purple. Matter whose touch
is intangible
defines who I am—no, inscrutable death
is impregnable.
What I'm saying I don't know, so I let the flower
come to me—not like
music to an ear, but like love to an unclean saint.

In No

time, I complete the process
of putting gas in my car, as, far

in the solar, wind-powered, electric
night, a man not just like me goes inside

to pay for charging. I miss me, and so
the legal tenderness between me and

the Shell station cashier is a shell
thrown by the same shore-powered wave, as

I pray far ahead to me upon one star
and the earth I haven't been to yet,

being not born, being born into
the earth I've poisoned almost beyond

repair. I don't miss me at all. Confused
beyond confusion, back outside now,

I wish we could cross over the sun's
trillions of edges, and start a new day.

Each Stage

of my life breaks imperfect
silence, learns like God to pray
back, to shine up like the sun,
is relentlessly forgotten.
Which means remembered?

I should mow the lawn,
or call someone on the phone
to replace a broken window,
instead of spinning abstractions.
My life seems to go

constantly from mental
to physical and back. Just once,
I'd like to go from mental
to mental, to cross and cross
over to a place where

fruition comes to, like consciousness
breaking off from a brain stem.
Instead of mowing the lawn,
or waiting as if for my phone
to call back, I should weed

the garden I don't have, pray
for a life I won't have one day
to go on spinning, and go
right to sleep on a flower
bed, or a bed.

The Collected Poems of Chris Waterson

My Mother's Letters

I've never been able to put my thoughts down
in any kind of order.
I think it's strange
that my father, who lives in a trailer park
outside San Francisco, thinks it strange
that I live in a city and breathe air
as one might breathe death.

I keep my mother's letters
in the file cabinet she bought me long ago,
when I was in high school.
I'm afraid to touch them.
She awakens from the dead
to tell me her ears are like seashells—
a sad, unoriginal image.

She asks me to write down
everything in her letters
that warmed my heart or
made my eyes water.

My eyes *are* water.
No one made them.

To Kirsten

When you said goodbye,
I tried to be kind
to myself. I wiped my eyes
carefully, so as to wound them,
but not kill them.
That night, I read myself
a story, but every character was me.
I closed the book,
rocked in my rocking chair.
Nothing worked,
you kept saying goodbye.

I could see the inside of your mouth.
I'm telling you
I refused to close your eyes.
I slept, your hand
on my hair, my head
against your shoulder.

They

They call it a fingernail moon.
They call it snow—each flake is the same
if you don't look too hard.
I'm taking a walk alone.
I forget the name of this street.
I'm tempted to put a snowball down my back,
but pain is bearable
only if it's a surprise.
A few days ago, I bought some new boots.
My feet are like two small fires.
I wish I could warm my hands over them.

For Failure

I have nothing to say.
I seem to write to fail,
and to have compassion
for failure,
as I have compassion for a little child
with a scraped knee, with no water,
no Band-Aid, no mother,
no soothing words.

The Ocean

I drive to the country, stop the car,
and begin to walk.

A fallen tree in the shape of a bear
is not what I'm looking for,
but I see it and rejoice.
It's so unusual, so alone.

I reach a waterfall, cup my hands,
plunge them in,
pull them out, and drink.

I have a long way to go.
I try to see through the force
with which a river moves
out of itself and crosses the ocean like a small boat.

Journal Entry

There it is:
the moon.
(I cannot really see it.)
It is never beyond comprehension,
but it is too late,
not the moon, not complete darkness,
just: It is too late.
Naturally, I think of the sun,
but no, it is not that common
to think of the sun
when the moon has risen
and will stay
for as long as we can bear it.
The sun astonishes us
with its senseless beauty.
Why disappear?
Why starve yourself?
We cherish the sun
as if it is food.
Do we?
Do we walk closer to it
and look into its eyes?
It matters whether we do or not.
Am I looking into its eyes
right now?
My door is closed.
My window is open just enough
for a breath of wind.
The light is on.
I remember flipping the switch
when I opened the door,
though it was light outside.
Irony is inevitable and finished.
The walls are as smooth as cut grass.
I am figuratively hungry.
It cannot be helped.
I grope for more light
than darkness can provide,
for the constant bright sun,
for the words I have and have not written.

CONCRETE

August 4, 2014

Because world war, the idea, the execution,
officially spawned 100 years ago
today, today

I will think like a trout, and head
upriver, even
under countless layers, perfectly smooth, of ice

I will keep going, thrashing through underwater
rapids, resting at times, not content,
intent

on reaching the place where I will
lay one egg,
and not two, and certainly not three.

The Reagan Era

It was superb, the song. It was superb.
Half-awake, coming to half-terms
with the tiny room cut in half
by the presence of the possessions
of my roommate gone for the weekend,
the rain done, the year, 1982,
beginning to fall, I brimmed over
with how I didn't know to what extent
the air shaft behind my head and outside
our one window was physical.
I was with the small but tiny
building on 112th and Broadway,
inside it, just as without question,
or with certainty, I was inside
my freshman year of college in
New York City, by my side, alone
on a Sunday morning after a late night
with friends, an overripe Saturday
involving fermented laughter and
varying liquids involving more
than the need to end thirst. And
I didn't know if the building's missing
wide spine consisted of air or
of a woman's throat, the two ends
of an Adam's apple suspended
in an arc over a smooth surface.
Privileged and hungry for unseen,
universal riches swinging low
over wages and charity
and a chariot (wrong song), was I
half-dreaming? To what extent?
Was I reverting back to dreaming
of waking to a world with its inside
scooped out so that half of its windows,
the lucky ones nestled away
from the streets, could breathe, though closed?
The one behind my head, I realized
or fantasized, was open all the way,
given the late September heat,
and a dead woman (I called her

"Judy," which was her exact name)
with a "Garland" of flowery, leafy,
precise softness at the top of her lungs,
was singing, going on and "Over"
about "the Rainbow" like a drunken child
wreathed with brain stems and freed cells.
It was superb. I was awake now,
to the music and the prank, no doubt
someone a few floors down half-
dangling his stereo speakers
out his window, laughing and blasting
sleepers from their slumbers
at such an ungodly hour, the music
and not the prank reverberating
and exploding like an immense,
contained throat. It was superb,
with just Judy hovering above
the source in a disembodied building,
an immense, upside-down glass of rain
with no ceiling or floor, her lit throat
whispering like a roar around my ears
and inner lids, having broken through the airy
glass behind my head, her lit throat arriving
too early to be wrong, given
the sun's multibright wish to never awaken
without chord changes and milked and nursed
syllables, the perfect world an upside-
down smile nuzzling the brutal streets,
tenderly belting out flesh and money,
deprivation, sleep, and the dream
that years later, there would be
conscious and conscionable peace
at last, if not where I would be,
then somewhere.

2008

October 24, 1929

It's said a murmuring
rose from the crowds of men
both outside and inside
the Stock Exchange, a mur-
muring like subdued fire
crackling just like cows
moaning or slaughtering
their own horror, trying
to...indescribable,
the way money is
and isn't life, the way
higher, even higher
speculative bubbles
burst before and after
turning all the way back
into descending jelly-
fish pumping, churning years
of water in vain, salt
in men's veins, leading to
bread and lines, better
than blood after and
before out of mouths
it rose, murmuring
something about savings
and lives of yellow fields
and red and yellow roses
(not even close),
murmuring in unison
a day before the brief
bank bailout, five whole
days before Black
Tuesday began, for lack
of another word, mur-
muring like both burnt
and unused coal both inside
and outside the earth.

Waiting for a Bank Machine

As I glare at the back of this woman
taking forever out of ignorance or inexperience,
I contemplate this miracle we inhabit,
continents big enough for two,
islands big enough for two,

volcanoes tall enough for two,
icebergs, one bank machine,
cold snaps, fault lines,
two needs,

and try to imagine that, instead of numbers,
she's punching in words: "Heaven, I grant you,
is desirable, but think of how, before
a leaf falls out of your eyes, it drops
into your irises like a seed." Yes, I imagine

to me she's saying, "I see myself rising in your eyes,
in your estimation, the sun above you a supplicant, my life
and your life one blanket of leaves above the ground
underneath depleted trees, the sun above us
asking you to watch my back." I'm not bitter

that I have to wait so long. It's nice putting words
in her mouth, and at her fingertips, signifying
her place on Earth, and mine, and our relationship
to the seasons,
and to the cosmos,
and to death. I'm not bitter at all.

The IRS

My first real job
was with the IRS, opening envelopes
and sorting the contents into categories.
On break, in the lunchroom, one fellow-

opener would say things to me like:
"Pretty boring work, isn't it?" and "Why
is life so cruel?" You must remember
she smiled as she talked. Her elegantly

styled hair made her ears stand out.
Her hands looked to me infinitesimally
raw and bruised, like children
who translate the words time

for bed as time for nightmares,
or like shy, awkward adolescents
who fit in nowhere, who can't take it,
pure and simple. She was married. Her clothes

looked beautiful on her. She would eat slowly,
hold an apple in both hands, for instance,
and breathe on it before taking a quiet bite.
Even now, she begins to laugh, motions to me,

points toward the trees beyond the window
and says things to me like: "Just think, there are
living things out there, and we're here inside,
making a living."

As I Apply for a Job

I have an urge
to see my body as an annex
in which someone like me
exists with closed windows
and unclear eyes, and a head and skull that turn
exquisite when they bow out of the world,
and then blood goes
beyond my skin once firm as fishbone,
and someone like me
has an urge to never

bleed again until the floor is drenched, and blood
is nothing more than clear water, and a door
exists through which
to enter the outside and clearly
perceive, in the weak light
of streetlights and headlights
(it's quitting time, and it's winter) that the chosen one
has gone under, drowned, but that both of us are walking
away toward the lives
we've been offered.

Self-Help

It's Monday night, and a car is blocking the dumpster
with the DO NOT BLOCK ON MONDAY NIGHT sign on it.
And there was never any hope that things would go as hoped.

Walking home from my job I wanted, on the morning of day one,
to love, I might as well be putting a book over my heart and allowing
the bullet through anyway. There was never any hope for such a thing

as being born to be ecstatic about everything.
The traffic at this intersection is just terrible. The little store
sells beer to minors. I'm out of gum. I refuse to go in there,

where the light of the world is so dim.
God knows when you're in a rotten mood
you should just examine your knuckles,

as much as your skin will allow, get home
from your job or wherever you've been
and sit down and examine your invisible

prowess. Then feel how your closed eyes
see through your bloodscreen to your blood.
Then, eyes still closed, look outward toward the green field.

What is it? Not green. Not a field. Then put your hands
over your eyelids. You've never been so dying
to read what the lines on your palms have to say.

The joy you were granted won't materialize, it will sing.

My Weekday Morning Routine

Night didn't stick, and so I went on living,
as if woke up
to the border between two peaceful countries
I had crossed
on the backs of five animals who declined
to comprehend
that the earth was one earth. Metaphor was like
the silhouette
of a pattern of renegade veins, and five loose
vials of blood,
and work was like the full length of a chick's beak
splitting wide
open five cracks in an egg. A half an hour later,
as I always
do, I drove 15 minutes, and then stopped, as
I do always,
at a particular store for coffee and breakfast.
There it was,
the counter, as well as the usual quite pleasant
young woman
behind it. I was sure—I mean I believe now—
that even
prior to dawn, she had been upright and alert,
counting,
over and over, her "thank yous." As soon as
she realized
that she had already said it once to me, she
apologized,
needlessly. She said it twice to me. That's how

it broke,
my weekday morning routine.

Aftereffect

Global warming is no longer a philosophical threat, no longer a future threat, no longer a threat at all. It's our reality.
   —Bill McKibben, *eaarth*

This morning, my coat on, I drove to work
through cold sunlight, and thought about our
reality, the result of doing without first
thinking, and tried to, around my brain, wrap
human-centered weather around the core
of an orange held in a primate's hand, and
asked myself how this could have happened,
and asked myself why doing is sometimes aberrant—
is that the right way to put it? This morning,
I longed for last night, for the imaginary
field that wasn't a vacant lot, for the field
that, already white, turned even more.
Last night, it was as if weather is never
aberrant, as if being cold is never wrong,
even when snow falls sideways and touches
a bare neck, even though a scarf was right there
for the taking on a rack in a front hallway.
Last night, coat and hat on, I walked on concrete
through cold rain to the nearby drugstore
to buy a few things, streetlights on, but no
streetlights illuminating a vacant lot, and
thought about drawing a small animal's brain
in such a way that it looked like an orange,
and of how if I did, I wouldn't know if
I should make it peeled or not, and of how
if I had the power to make an orange
even smaller, and put it inside a small
animal's head, it wouldn't be like slipping
a tooth under a pillow, or like anything at all.
No, all that never happened inside my head, even
though it could have, since thinking is never aberrant—
does that make sense? What did happen was this:
Twice, I tilted my head back, letting the uncovered
half of my forehead touch rain, letting rain
take the warmth that outer skin wishes to yield,
and the starless sky fell back on its reality,
like a blanket of snow sliding onto a white field.

Two Months After the Partial Clear-Cutting Across the Road from My House

Our moods do not believe in each other,
according to Emerson, and I
believe him, not in yesterday's
remorse as I looked into
the mere distance, and saw
some winter fir trees.

What Emerson called
the law of eternal
procession I sacrifice
to a separate branch of myself
limited to today. To my joy,
some fir trees annexed their rings, did not die.

Forecast

Because to appreciate
the natural world is to lament its swift decline
over the last
hundred years or so, on miraculous water
I not only walk,
but also stand still.

What am I saying?
Rain is still until it falls, I tell myself, as if
pressing a depreciated
leaf—mint or maple—branched off from an expired,
but not tired,
plant or tree—between two fingers, mine,
or my other hand's.

Rain is
still until I listen
to it drinking from the roots of the tender young shoots,
but not tendrils,
of an elongated plant, or a minute tree, testing,
but not tasting,
the dead air, and falling and falling through it,
and adding,

all around me, nothing
new. Now I fathom all I can rely on when I rely on
the slow, so
slow, almost time-lapsed, natural world.
When, unlike the world,
I run and stand still.

Poem to a Friend

I didn't know
what to say when you told me over the phone
that on a camping trip
over the weekend your dog ran off a cliff.
I pictured
your dog standing on air for the longest moment.
Such is life, as is
shedding tears over a cartoon in which
the ground on which
the end of falling will soon take place is as
soft as bones.
The edge went on forever, according to
your dog's more than
sound eyesight.
Mistaken instinct isn't much of an
explanation.
It's more
like: The edge clearly wasn't wide enough, and then
began to go
on being the edge in the insubstantial irises
of a bodiless dog.
Who knows
why everything disappears when the flesh-feigning sun rises?
It drowns,
an otter's stomach, as its hungry chest acts as a plate.
Who knows?
An otter, its almost
hands like half-shells...
It falls, one
of a nameless species of bird, as it leaves the edge for
the chance to reach an
upper register only you can hear, only you, your
two hands, in
disbelief, over a cliff face filled with spiders threading
crevices together, before
your fingertips ran down and away from your forehead,
your fingerbones
down and away from your eyes, your soft palms

down and away from your mouth,
and then I knew
what to say, but couldn't even begin
to say it.

Acknowledgments

Grateful acknowledgment is made to the following journals, where these poems first appeared, sometimes in slightly different versions.

2River: "Detail Study," "Prime Dream"
Agave: "Forgivable"
Alluvian: "Aftereffect"
Body: "A Walk Through Central Park"
The Bookends Review: "Forecast," "Monday Morning Logic," "Self-Help"
The Broadkill Review: "To a Stranger," "Pop Song"
Burnside Review: "Where I Live," "Poem to a Friend"
Canada Quarterly: "The Valley of," "Gone Now," "The Days of My Birth"
Cacti Fir: "The Life of the Mind," "The IRS"
Chariton Review: "Deliberate Ecstasy"
The Comstock Review: "Waiting for a Bank Machine"
Foliate Oak: "My Weekday Morning Routine"
Free State Review: "Pigeon"
GFT: "Children's Poem"
Ginosko Literary Journal: "First Love," "Modern Romance," "Pre-Valentine's Day Poem," "The Young Man," "The House Where We Used to Live"
The Hollins Critic: "Self-Portrait"
Ironwood: "A Dream," "Journal Entry"
The Louisville Review: "As I Apply for a Job"
Matter: "The Reagan Era"
OccuPoetry: "October 29, 1929"
The Ocotillo Review: "The Not Me"
Pamplemousse: "Inorganic," "Symphony in One Movement"
Paperbark: "In No," "Two Months After the Partial Clear-Cutting Across the Road from My House"
The Plum Creek Review: "The Process"
Potomac Review: "Metaphysical Siblings"
Poydras Review: "The Foundation"
Tipton Poetry Journal: "A Visitor," "Exterior Interior Monologue"
The Tulane Review: "Sonnet"
West Texas Literary Review: "August 4, 2014"

About the Author

Douglas Nordfors is a native of Seattle, and has lived since 1989 in and around Charlottesville, Virginia. He has a BA from Columbia University (1987) and an MFA in poetry from the University of Virginia (1991), and has taught writing and literature at Milton Academy, the University of Virginia, James Madison University, Germanna Community College, and other places. Beginning in 1987, he has published poems in numerous journals, including "Quarterly West," "California Quarterly," "Poetry Northwest," "The Iowa Review," "Poet Lore," "The Hampden-Sydney Poetry Review," "The Seattle Review," and "The Sycamore Review." Plain View Press published his two previous books of poetry, *Auras* (2008) and *The Fate Motif* (2013). He is also a fiction writer, with three so-called "literary" novels self-published and available online, *Jane Davies, Little Book*, which is based on the early life of Ralph Waldo Emerson, and *Wokokon*.

www.ingramcontent.com/pod-product-compliance
Lightning Source LLC
Chambersburg PA
CBHW050042080526
44586CB00014B/1416